Best Ever
Play-and-Learn
Sticker
Collection

HERMES
HOUSE

contents

My Day at Home

Can you find the
skipping Teddy Bear?

Who is just waking up?

Do you like painting
pictures?

Can you see the bear
taking a bath?

Who is sitting doing
nothing?

Can you see the
yellow clock?

Getting up

I wonder what will happen today?

7 o'clock

Who else is getting out of bed?

Rise and shine!

a big stretch

Breakfast time! Hungry puppies first...

then toys...

...and now I can have my breakfast.

I am wearing my orange dungarees.

chest of drawers

Can you find my shoes and jacket?

My hair is in pigtails so that it doesn't get in my eyes.

I am ready to face the day.

A busy morning
We're out and about today.

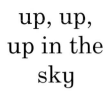

up, up,
up in the
sky

Let's go to
the park
and feed
the
ducks.

Can you find some
ducks to eat our
chunks of bread?

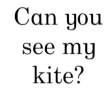

Can you
see my
kite?

Where are
the ducks?

Quack, quack!

Do you wear armbands or goggles when you go swimming?

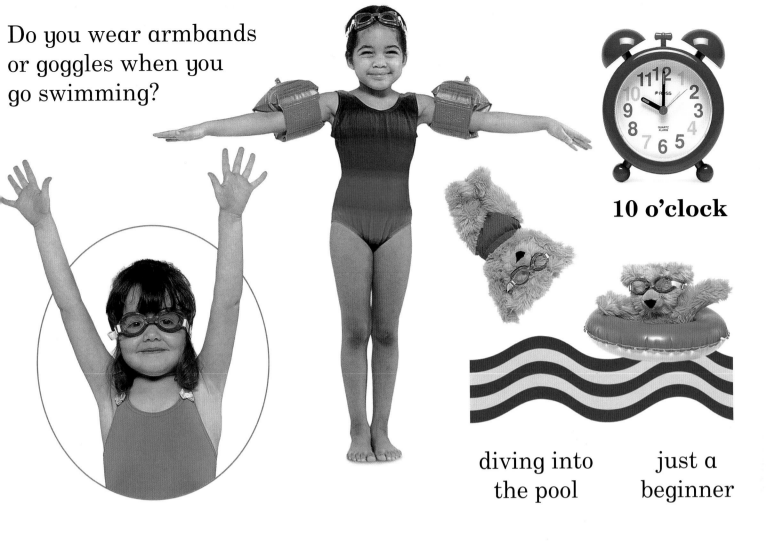

10 o'clock

diving into the pool

just a beginner

It's time to go home and bake some cakes.

This green icing tastes good!

Can you find five cakes to cool on the wire rack?

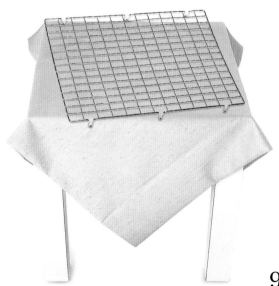

9

Playing with friends

Later in the morning my friends come round to play.

Where are my friends hiding?

Shhh!

"Ting!" goes the triangle.

"Crash!" go the cymbals.

Who else is in the band?

Tom and Sam are playing a fishing game. Find some more fish for them.

11 o'clock

How many green fish has Tom caught?

How many red fish has Sam caught?

fun with facepaints

It's picnic time for my teddy bears.

11

Lunchtime

It's half past 12. Time to have something to eat and drink.

This orange juice is delicious.

Can you find more orange juice and milk for the children?

I like creamy cold milk.

Open wide!

My lunch is packed in a box.

This dragon is eating broccoli for lunch.

Eleanor is eating a cheese sandwich.

Half past 12

Can you put some fruit on the plate for her to eat afterwards?

After lunch, James washes up.

Would you like a cookie?

Someone's eaten them all!

In the garden

It's hot this afternoon.

I can bounce.

I can't.

Ted and
I go
exploring.

What am I growing?

I am going
to water
my flowers
to make
them grow.

I have a slide in my garden.

2 o'clock

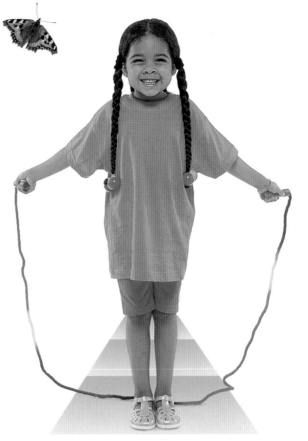

Skipping is hard to learn, but it's fun.

Who else is learning to skip?

I am watching the creepy-crawlies in my garden. Can you make a line of snails on the wall?

can make lots of
ess with sand in
the garden.

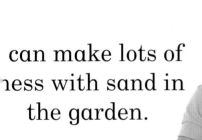

Back indoors

There's lots to do inside as well.

3 o'clock

Frog and Bear are painting.

Do you like my picture? It's hard to keep inside the lines.

Can you find some more paints?

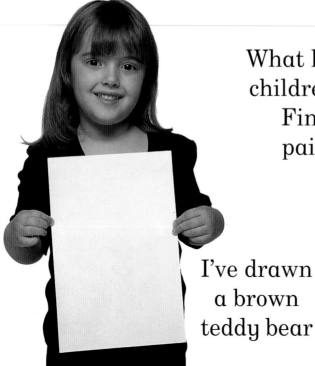

What have these children drawn? Find their paintings.

I've drawn a brown teddy bear

My picture is of purple grapes

16

This tower
is tall.

Can you find a
clock? What
time is it now?

I'm building a castle.

Put blocks on this tower
until it is even taller.

Dragon and I
are doing a
jigsaw puzzle.

Brrm!
Brrm!

Jessica is
reading a
story.

Where
does this
piece go?

Getting ready for bed

It's been a busy day. Now it's time to get ready to go to bed.

6 o'clock

Let's read a bedtime story.

It's bathtime. Can you find some toys for Alice?

a big bubbly bath for the bears

A big soft towel will soon get Alex dry.

I mustn't forget to clean my teeth.

Sleepyhead

It's time to say goodnight.

7 o'clock

Can you find the blind to cover the window?

Everyone's asleep.

What a big yawn!

"Good night, Leah."

"Sweet dreams, Matt."

We'll be ready for another busy day tomorrow.

19

Kitchen

This is the room where we cook our food.

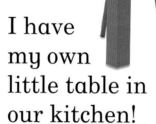

I have my own little table in our kitchen!

We're cooking. Put some ingredients on the table.

spatula

whisk

Look at all these kitchen things.

cheese grater

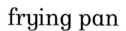

frying pan   saucepan

I'm eating an egg in the kitchen.

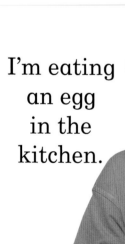

Find some more vegetables to wash in the colander.

Food is kept in the kitchen.

cheese

canned tuna

raisins

honey

pasta

jam

ketchup

It's time for tea. Can you find the teapot?

Cleaning can be fun!

What would you put in here?

Put the dirty dishes into the bowl.

Find some plates for me to dry.

21

Dining room

We eat our meals in the dining room.

I'm helping to set the table.
Can you find me some plates?

Find cups for these saucers.

snack time

a family meal

lunch

22 Add two more glasses.

Can you set another place for lunch?

Living room

We relax in the living room.

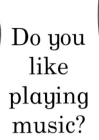

Flowers brighten up the room.

Do you like playing music?

reading together

squashy beanbag

This houseplant has shiny green leaves.

a quiet moment

comfy cushion

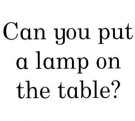

Can you put a lamp on the table?

Who likes to stretch out on the rug?

Bathroom
This is the cleanest room in the home.

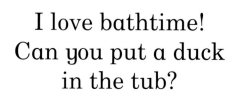

sponge crab

I love bathtime!
Can you put a duck in the tub?

Where's the toothbrush?

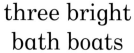

potty

red facecloth

three bright bath boats

I brush my teeth in the bathroom.

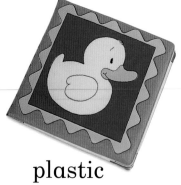

plastic bath book

soft bath towel

Put some more bath things on the shelf.

Baby's room

Some babies have
a room of their own.

elephant
mobile

teddy bear

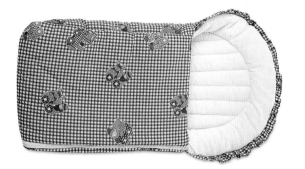

snuggly sleeping bag

baby's
bottle

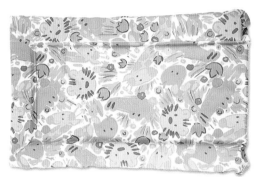

Look at all these
changing things.

Shhh! Don't wake
the sleeping baby.

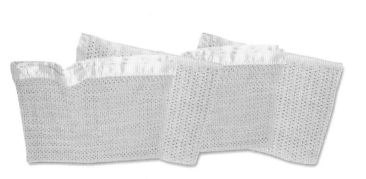

soft blankets

Find a baby getting ready. 25

Bedroom

This is the room where we sleep and dress.

Dragon has his own bed.

Shhh, it's bedtime.

bedroom lamp

This elephant never forgets the time.

Can you put some more books on the shelves?

I'm looking out of my bedroom window.

Can you put two teddy bears on the chair?

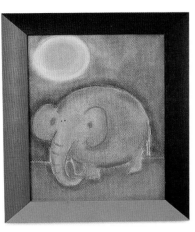

my bedroom
picture

dressing gown

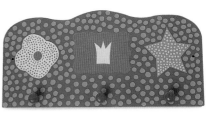

What would you
hang up here?

Can you find
the other
slipper?

I'm ready for
the day!

What do
you think
is inside?

bedroom
drawers

I've got to clean up my room!

Find another
sleepy head.   27

Playroom

Some children have a special room to play in.

Who's hiding behind the chair?

Can you find some more pencils?

Say goodnight to the teddy bears.

toy clock

Can you guess what we are dressed up as?

puzzle

hand puppet

Here you are, Big Bear.

How does Space Ted get home?

How many people are going to have tea?

paintbox

Let's cook.

Find some fun hats for these teddy bears.

We're not at home!

29

My garden

We can dig and grow flowers in the garden.

I like swinging in the garden.

Gardening can be messy.

How many flowers are there?

Do you grow flowers outside your window?

Fill the wheelbarrow with plants.

earth

garden broom

trowel

I'm watching my plants grow.

pretty pot plants

Have you got snails in your garden?

Find some flowers to put in these pots!

big green leaf

Can you find the missing red boot?

 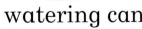

watering can

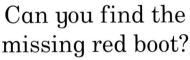

I have a garden pond. Can you find some more ducks?

I left my bike in the garden.

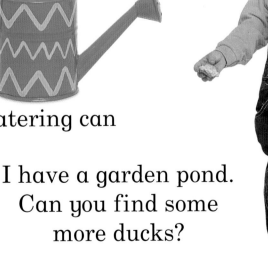

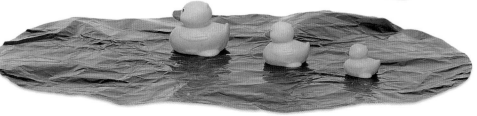

31

Toolshed

This is where grown-ups
keep their tools and paint.

I've got my
own toy
tool box.

screwdriver

hammer

nails

rope

saw

bolts

nut

sandpaper

copper
nails

Pile up
some
more
cans.

shiny
steel
nails

step ladder

Which room?

Find something to go
in the different rooms.

Who's cooking in the kitchen?

Find a funny
toy to keep the
baby happy.

What does
this cook
need?

Find some bread for
the dining room.

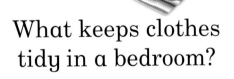

What keeps clothes
tidy in a bedroom?

Who's on the
beanbag in the
living room?

We're in the
playroom.
Is there
a hat
for me?

Which rooms do
these belong in? 33

Clothes

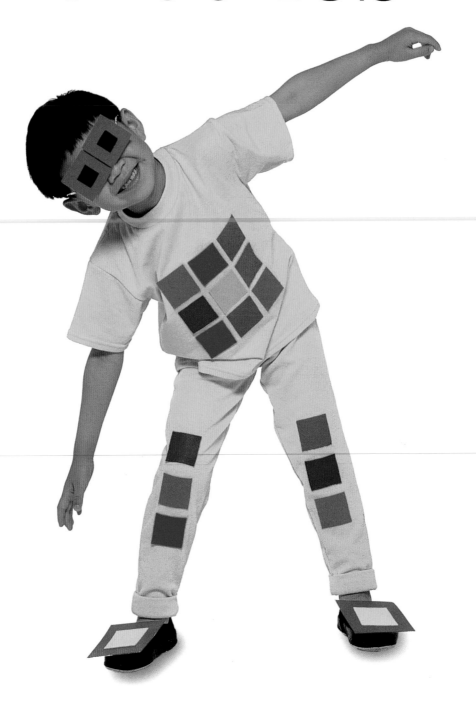

Who is ready to go out in
the rain?

Which toy is going
on holiday?

Find a doll wearing a
knitted dress.

Who's wearing a
pretty hair ribbon?

Can you see the boy
getting dressed?

What would you wear
in the cold?

Getting dressed

How many clothes can you put on all by yourself?

These are my dungarees.

First I put on my socks.

Next comes my shirt.

All ready to face the world.

Can you find some more clothes to put in the chest of drawers?

red t-shirt

shorts

orange t-shirt

socks

Where's my arm gone?

I don't want to get dressed!

Teddy Bear needs to get dressed too.

How do I put this on?

Can you find my clothes?

37

Patterns

It's fun to wear clothes that have different patterns.

I'm putting on a stripy t-shirt.

stripy cap

stripes going from side to side

stripes going up and down

Who else is wearing stripes?

Do you like the heart on my stripy dungarees?

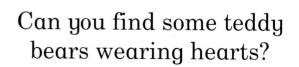

Can you find some teddy bears wearing hearts?

squares from top to bottom

This pattern is called checks.

tiny checks in red and white

Can you find three bears in cheerful checks?

Can you find more socks to put on the washing line?
What patterns are on the socks?

Keeping cool

In hot weather we wear clothes that are light and cool.

shorts

Can you find all the clothes to go in my suitcase?

sunglasses

shirt

beach shoes

cap

swimming trunks

sports shoes

t-shirt

I also need some warmer clothes for the evening.

I'm going on holiday too.

Swimming costumes are meant to get wet.

Who else is ready to splash around in the pool?

My cap shades my neck from the sun.

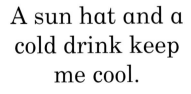

A sun hat and a cold drink keep me cool.

cool, flowery summer dress

41

Keeping warm and dry

We wear warm, waterproof clothes
when it's cold and wet outside.

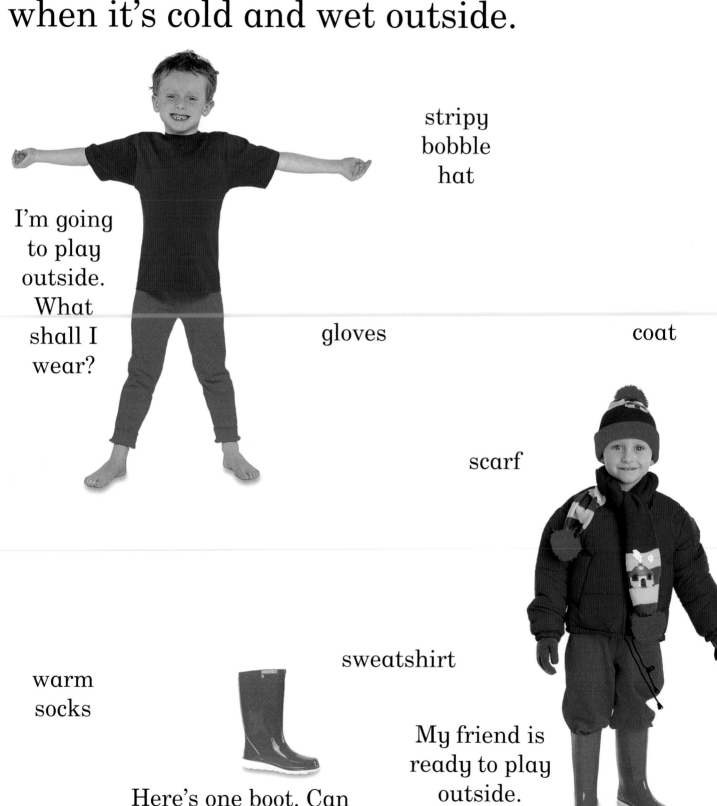

stripy
bobble
hat

I'm going
to play
outside.
What
shall I
wear?

gloves

coat

scarf

warm
socks

sweatshirt

Here's one boot. Can
you find the other?

My friend is
ready to play
outside.

42

I'm dressed for
wet weather.

What keeps you
dry in the rain?

rain hat

A yellow raincoat
keeps my fur dry.

umbrella

There
aren't any
clothes to
keep my
nose
warm.

Watch out!

43

Useful clothes

We have all sorts of clothes that are just right for different situations.

helmet

I don't mind if I fall off my skateboard!

elbow pads

knee pads

If I fall off my bike, I won't hurt my head.

Can you find more protective things to wear?

Aprons protect our clothes from glue.

goggles for swimming

catcher's glove for playing ball

My apron is
waterproof...

...and so are my gloves.

A bib stops my clothes
from getting too messy.

Can you find
my slippers?

I wear warm cosy
clothes to go to bed.

Where's my
dressing gown?

Special clothes
What do you like wearing best?

Add a flower to Daniel's t-shirt to make it really special.

I dance in my pretty pink dress.

Find another pet wearing a jacket.

warm black coat

Can you find me a sparkly collar?

Does orange suit me?

Find a pretty ribbon for each of the bears.

I'm a winner in my soccer kit.

My clothes look even better this way up!

Can you find Nellie in her pretty floaty skirt?

Find a flowery teddy bear.

Who is wearing a silver leotard?

I love my sweater because it feels so soft.

I become a superhero in my cape.

47

Oops!
Dressing up in the wrong clothes can be fun.

You're wearing MY t-shirt!

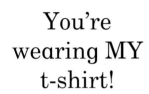

You're wearing MY t-shirt!

Find a dog wearing a big bow tie.

too wide

too small

too big

huge shoes

gigantic
glasses

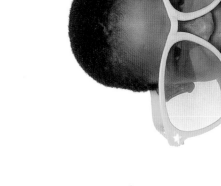

A skirt made
for two.

Find a dog wearing
a hair ribbon.

These are
too small
for Sean.

But they would be
just right for James.

I'm grown up!
Can you find
my hat?

49

Party

Hear the balloons go
BANG!

Which present would
you like?

Do you like dressing up?

Can you see lots of
balloons for the party?

Do you like playing
party games?

Who is wearing the
funny glasses?

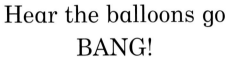

Getting ready

Let's prepare for a really fun party.

Making paper chains is fun!

How many colours can you find?

I love bright balloons.

I'm blowing up balloons.

Find some more balloons for the party.

Making food

It's time to make some tasty food for the party.

Let's start cooking!

Don't forget the icing.

I love to eat yummy cakes.

Can you find some more party treats?

We like party food.

Dressing up

Sometimes it is hard to decide what to wear for a party.

What shall I wear?

How about these clothes?

I thought this was a costume party!

Choose an outfit for Lucy.

Party time

There are lots of reasons to have a party!

Happy Birthday!

I'm having a Halloween party.

I love Christmas parties.

Crackers go BANG!

 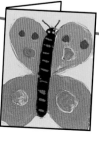  

Find some more birthday cards to complete the row.

55

Party cakes

There are many special cakes for parties.

We are dreaming of delicious party cakes.

Can you tell how old I am today?

Find the scary ghost cake.

Find the pretty birthday present cake.

I'm dreaming of a festive Christmas cake.

Find the delicious candy-covered cake.

What's inside this Christmas cake?

Find a birthday balloon cake to put on Ruth's plate.

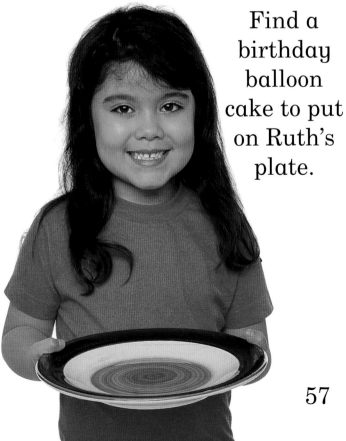

57

Lots of presents

It's fun to receive lots of presents at a party.

I'm ready for my present.

What do you think this could be?

I wonder what this is?

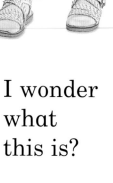

Which present would you like?

Find some more presents for the children.

Look at all the transport toys these children got for their birthdays.

I have a new train set.

Look at my new truck.

Ted and I are going for a ride.

I'm loading up the trailer.

Find some party hats for the children.

Fun and games

What games do you like to play at parties?

Time to play!

What can I find in the bag?

Abracadabra!

I will magic a teddy bear from this box.

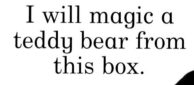

Wow!

Magic some flowers for the magician.

We're playing a whispering game.

Find some more apples for Anna.

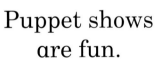

Puppet shows are fun.

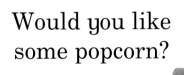

Would you like some popcorn?

61

Music and dance

Do you like listening to music at parties?

I'm playing the guitar.

I love to sing.

Let's play "Happy Birthday".

I love to rock and roll.

I like to swing and jive.

Dancing is a lot of fun.

Let's go up and down and all around.

Find some more musical instruments for the teddy bear party band.

63

Send in the clowns

Welcome, boys and girls, to the party clowns' fabulous circus!

I'm a happy clown.

Look out, Dragon!

This flower squirts water.

Find some more balls for the clown to juggle.

Time to go

It's time for the party children to go home.

Put all the toys away.

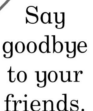

Say goodbye to your friends.

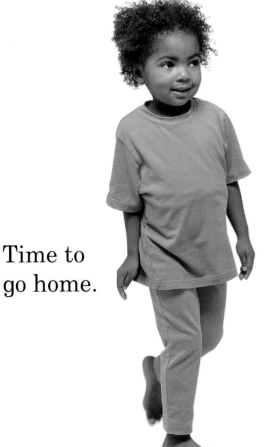

Get your skates on!

Time to go home.

Give all of the party children some treats to take home.

65

Food and Drink

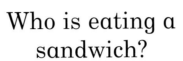

Who is eating a sandwich?

Can you find the girl drinking milk?

Who is baking cakes?

What is your favourite drink?

Do you like eating fish?

What food is on the plate?

What did you have for breakfast?

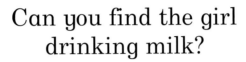

All sorts of food

Can you find some more sausages to sizzle in the pan?

slices of bacon

egg in a pan

little fat sausages

tasty eggs

crumbly cake

yummy cheese

delicious chocolates

juicy grapes

scaly silver fish

68

tiny green peas in a bowl

watermelon

Bright red and black
summer berries.

long
orange
carrots

Can you find all the
juicy fruits that are
in this bowl?

cool
green
cucumber

green-and-white
leek

round
brown
mushrooms

parsnip

sliced bread

Can you find some
other pretty
peppers?

Find the chunky sandwich
the teddy bear has made.

69

Mealtimes

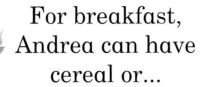

For breakfast, Andrea can have cereal or...

...bread

...jam

...an egg

For lunch, Samantha eats a sandwich.

Rebecca makes a salad.

Can you find three tomatoes for Rebecca and one for Samantha?

Big Ted and Little Ted are thirsty. Can you find them each a drink?

messy
spaghetti

delicious
raspberry
mousse

sticky
toffee
treat

I'm
singing for
my supper!

Can you put
a tasty meal
on Rachel's
plate?

We eat our evening meal
at the table.

71

Drinks to cool you down

On a hot day, orange juice is refreshing.

I love drinking cold milk.

Ice makes drinks cooler.

tasty orange juice

Frozen orange juice makes an orange ice. Can you find some more?

Can you give a refreshing treat to each teddy bear?

Drinks to warm you up

Scruffy old bear likes tea and cake. Can you find some funny-face cupcakes?

This drink is all mine.

two coffee cups

fresh coffee

teapot

We love to drink hot chocolate.

two tea mugs

Let's look in the kitchen

Hungry teddy bear wants to eat French fries.

Find a pan to cook with.

Can you find a happy meal for this sad teddy bear?

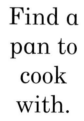

oven-baked pizza

Yuk! I hate pizza ... can you find me seven crunchy cookies instead?

dried pasta and rice

Find the mugs and bowls to place on the shelf too.

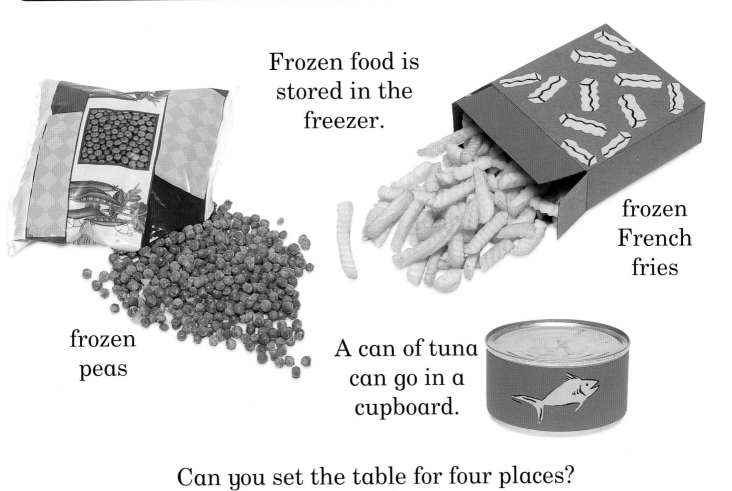

Frozen food is stored in the freezer.

frozen French fries

frozen peas

A can of tuna can go in a cupboard.

Can you set the table for four places?

Let's bake cakes!

flour

baking tin

butter

eggs

sugar

scales

Whisk the ingredients together.

Baking cakes together is fun!

Delicious!

Can you find the teddy bear's whisk?

rolling pin

Can you find an apron and a spoon?

cooling rack

This pink and green icing tastes sweet!

I'm the best chef!

Can you find the big cake that the teddy bear baked?

Food shapes

spiral
cake

Four small squares of cake
make one big square.

oval
eggs

star
fruit

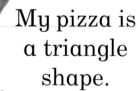

round apple

ring
cookies

My pizza is
a triangle
shape.

rectangular
toast

square
sliced
bread

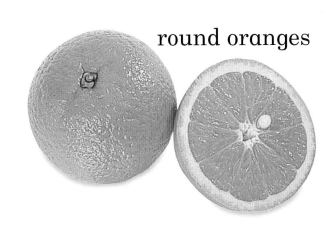

round oranges

Find a
wrapped
chocolate
triangle.

Can you find
another star
cookie?

lemon
semi-circles

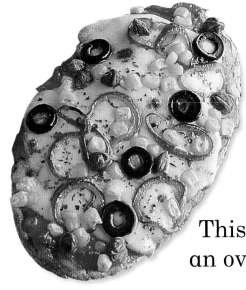

Can you find five
more diamond
sweets?

This pizza is
an oval shape.

79

Strange food and drink

Two bright pink desserts.

Yuk! Would you eat blue mashed potato?

What does this food taste like, Alice?

A pile of purple noodles!

You don't eat spaghetti with your feet!

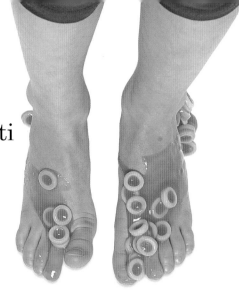

Have you ever seen a red hamburger?

Six long, blue carrots.

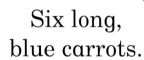

Heather is wearing a blindfold. Can she tell what her drink is?

Can you add silver peas to the plate?

Babies and Toddlers

Can you find the chick?

Who is playing with the big
beach ball?

Do you wear a sunhat?

Can you touch your toes?

Look out for the
mischief-makers!

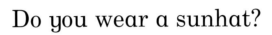

Find the baby sitting in
the swing

Where's the teddy bear?

All sorts of babies

I can see happy babies, sleepy babies and one crying baby.

Please pick me up.

Who can I see in the mirror?

I'm so happy to see you.

I have two puppies. Where have they gone?

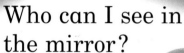

Can you find my chicks?

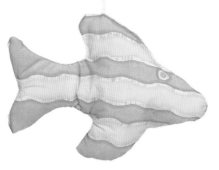

I watch the mobile go round and round.

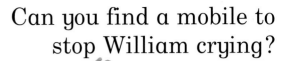

Can you find a mobile to stop William crying?

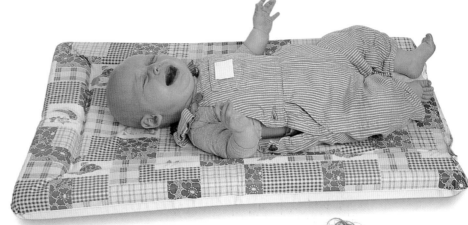

This tastes good.

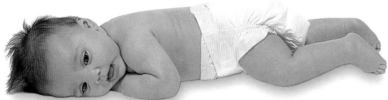

I'll just have a rest, and then I'll be ready to play.

I'm happy in my bouncy chair.

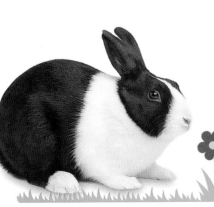

Can you find my babies?

85

Baby's room

What a lot of things babies have.

Look at all the things I've found.

Babies sleep under soft blankets. Can you find some to put by the cot?

What's this? What else do you need to change a baby?

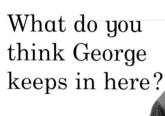

baby wipes

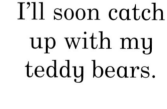

changing mat

What do you think George keeps in here?

I'll soon catch up with my teddy bears.

Find the other teddy bear.

Getting dressed

Babies wear soft comfortable clothes.

How do I put all these clothes on?

Now the shoes.

I like wearing red clothes.

Can you find me some bootees to wear?

Find another teddy bear who likes wearing red.

I like wearing yellow clothes.

Can you find me some bootees too?

Who's this?

Babies love hiding and playing disguises.

I can't see you.

baby in disguise

Who can I see?

I'm hiding behind a great big ball.

Hello, Ted.

Who is in the pushchair?

Peek-a-boo!

Here's Harry!

Whose nose is this?
Can you find the
right sticker?

Look at Jack's hat!

Can you see me hiding
behind the train?

Can you find
a real rabbit?

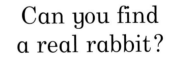

We're both
rabbits.

89

On the move

Babies and toddlers never sit still.

I'm off to see the world.

We'll come too.

We're dancing to the music. Can you find the band playing for us?

Can
someone
give me
a push?

I'm just
hanging
around.

Find more kittens to join in the game.

Caught it!

seesaw
sisters

Shall we
play ball?

Clever babies

Look at all the things these babies have learned to do.

I'm looking at the pictures.

Listen to my rattle. Can you find me another one?

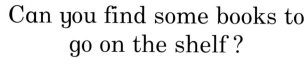

Can you find some books to go on the shelf?

Books are fun.

Big dragon reads a story to Baby dragon.

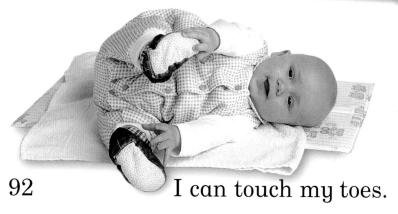

I can touch my toes.

Can you find a teddy bear who can touch his toes?

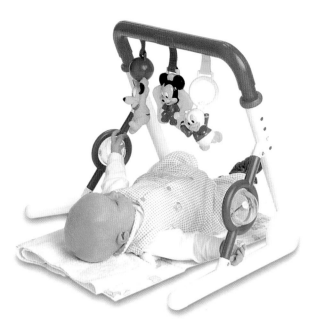

I can reach
the mobile.

What does this do?

painting
lesson

I'll need some
more rings. Can
you find them
for me?

I can make the
truck move.

I'm the Queen!

93

Mischief-makers

Oh, no! What are these
naughty babies doing?

I've spilled some paint.
Can you see it?

painting
the floor

Oh, no!
Look at
this
mess.

yellow
scribbles

What have you
done, kitty?

I'm throwing
all the
balls out
of the box.

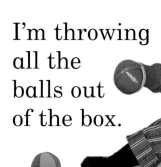

I'm a little devil.

We're splashing around.

Shhh!

We're making
a very loud
noise.

two messy
eaters

I'm thirsty. Can you
find me a drink?

Can you find me a
clean bib?

95

Baby's day
Look at all the things we do in a day.

waking up

getting changed and dressed

playing with toys

Look what I've found.

Can you find my toys?

96

eating

Can you find some cakes
to put on the plate?

exploring

It's time to feed the puppies.

Can you find
a bowl of food
and a bone for
each puppy?

Shhh! Goodnight, Baby.

bathtime

97

Animals and Nature

Which insects have wings?

What noise does a pig make?

How many legs does the spider have?

Which animal slithers along the ground?

Can you see a purple flower?

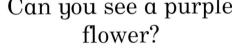

Which animal would you keep as a pet?

Which of these things might you see in a wood?

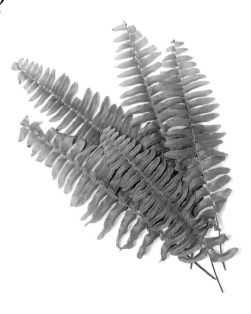

All sorts of animals
Meet the birds, beasts, fish and bugs

furry
cuddly cats

swimming orange fish

lovable
long-eared
dog

funny green
lizard

spotted
bugs

shiny
hopping
frogs

many-legged
centipede

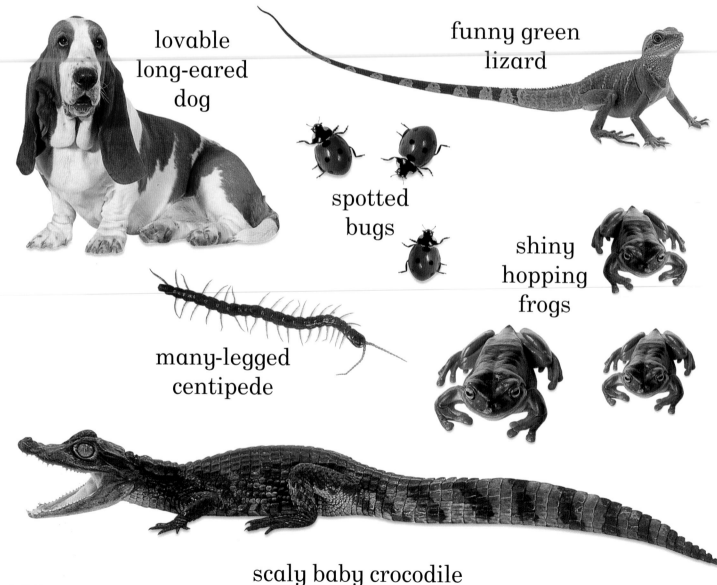

scaly baby crocodile

strong black-and-
white horse

Can you find
the dog who
owns this tail?

patterned
butterfly

creepy
crawling
spiders

Ella and James love
their pet rabbits.

slow plodding
tortoise

beady-eyed
eagle

101

On the farm
Who lives on a farm?

The goat has a tufty beard and a short tail.

The hen lays eggs in a nest for us to eat.

The sheep has a thick coat we can use to make wool.

Can you collect three more eggs to add to the nest?

The cow chews hay and grass to make milk for us to drink.

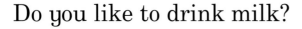

Do you like to drink milk?

Even small
ponies can
be very
strong.

Find a pink friend
for this black pig.

The cockerel has
a red comb.

The wise owl
keeps watch from
the post.

The proud duck has lost
her three ducklings.
Can you find them for her?

103

Animal homes
Where do my animal friends live?

A nesting box for a bird family. Decorate the birdbox with pretty stickers.

The puppy sleeps in his basket.

I live in my shell.

Bees live in a beehive. Can you find some more buzzing bees for each flower?

Look who's coming in through the cat door!

Who lives in this cage?

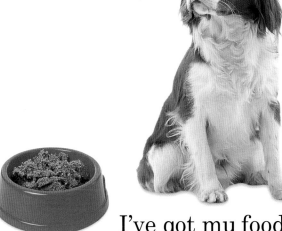

I've got my food but where is my kennel?

Put the cat in her basket.

I'm the king of the castle!

My home is warm and cosy.

Where is our hutch?

105

Dinner time
Animals get hungry just like we do.

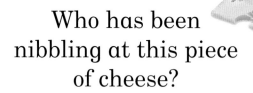

Who has been nibbling at this piece of cheese?

These greedy puppies are always very hungry.

Can you find a piece of cheese to feed each hungry mouse?

I wonder what Spot would like for dinner...

This tastes delicious.

This horse likes to eat hay.

Where is my water bucket?

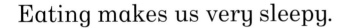

Eating makes us very sleepy.

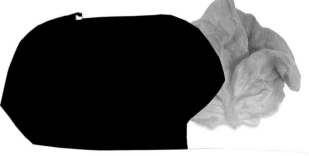

Guinea pigs like to nibble on juicy lettuce leaves and gulp water from a bottle.

Rabbits like to munch on crunchy carrots.

Can you find some more food and drink for these animals?

107

Playtime!

Animal friends love to play.

It's time to wake up and play! Find some toys to play with.

You won't catch us!

Where are the mice running to?

Jackie takes her puppy for an afternoon walk.

These puppies have lost their squeaky toy bones. Can you find them?

Teddy bear is my best friend.

I want to go for a walk!

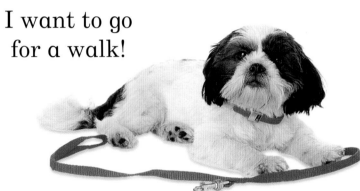

The kitten is having fun with a ball of string.

Can you find some more toys for the animal friends?

Look for three more tortoises to join in the race. Who is winning?

Animal noises

pigs say oink

cows say moo

bees buzz

cats say miaow

mice squeak

sheep say baa

horses neigh

dogs say woof

Can you make these animal noises too?

110

Baby animals

A baby cow is called a calf.

A baby cat is called a kitten.

This dog has three baby puppies.

A baby hen is called a chick.

A baby pig is called a piglet.

Can you find some friends for the baby animals?

Party animals!

The animals are having a party.

See how many balls you can balance on the crocodile's nose.

The puppies are inviting all their friends.

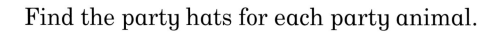

Find the party hats for each party animal.

The cats are dancing to the music.

Find some dancing partners for the wriggling worms.

Can I join the party too?

I'm joining in with the animals' party!

The sheep likes to party.

You can join in too!

Weather

Look at the different types of weather.

We like sunbathing.

sunny day

Find an animal that likes to sunbathe.

We're dressed for wet weather.

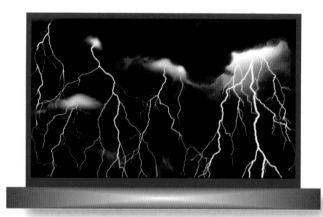

stormy night

Worms like wriggling in wet grass. Look for another one.

Can you find a duck to paddle in the puddle?

windy day

Find another
bird to glide
on the wind.

The wind has
made my hair
all messy.

Look for
more leaves
to blow in
the wind.

I like playing
in the snow.

Penguins come
from a snowy
place called the
South Pole. Can
you find another
penguin?

snowy day

Naturally beautiful

Look around you and see all the different shapes and sizes in nature.

red
flower

orange
flower

purple
flower

Can you find the
yellow flower?

red
grapes

green grapes

yellow
banana

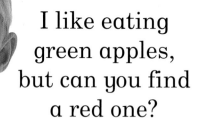

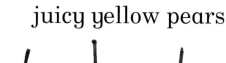

Put some more
red strawberries
in the box.

I like eating
green apples,
but can you find
a red one?

juicy yellow pears

Make another line of pears.

Butterflies and moths have pretty and delicate wings.

Find a butterfly that looks like me.

Watch out! It's a stripy snake.

The parrot's feathers are very bright.

A juicy green insect was sitting on that branch. Where has it gone?

117

Nature at home

Look around your home and you'll find lots of living things.

Find some more plants to put on the table.

I wish I could reach those pesky flies.

My fishy friend can breathe underwater.

My friend has escaped. Can you find her?

My puppy is tired from playing all day.

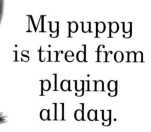

Nature on your doorstep

Let's find out what's in the garden.

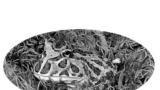

Are there any
more plants for
us to grow in
our garden?

We're playing leap-frog.
Can you find our playmate?

Follow the bees to the honey.

Find some more
creepy-crawlies
for creepy-
crawly corner.

Who will win this
race? The rabbit,
the tortoise or
the snail?

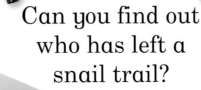

Can you find out
who has left a
snail trail?

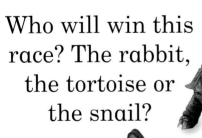

In the woods

Let's go for a walk in the woods and see what we can find.

The wise old owl lives in the woods.

A dragonfly darts through the woods, looking for sunny spots.

Find a butterfly that would like to drink from this flower.

Some trees drop their leaves when the weather gets cold.

Pine cones contain seeds that will grow into new trees.

Nuts are seeds, too. Find another brown nut.

Mushrooms grow in the soil.

Find some animals to live in this huge tree.

squirrel

owl

chipmunk

These are the leaves of a plant called a fern.

Tiny seedlings grow into big trees.

Can you find a woodland insect with lots of legs?

Complete the line of marching ants.

121

On the farm

Cock-a-doodle-doo! Let me show you around my farm.

Can you see the goat's wispy beard and short tail?

I eat lots of hay and make milk for you to drink. Try to find some hay for my dinner.

Horses have long, strong legs to help them run and jump.

Fox is hiding. Can you find him?

I've lost my chicks. Try to find them before the fox does.

Let's feed the ducks some bread.

It's my job to keep the sheep together.

QUACK!

QUACK!

QUACK!

Can you find the lost sheep?

A female pig is called a sow.

I am a farmer.

Put some toy cows into the pen.

123

Walk on the wild side

See how many different wild animals you can spot.

Elephants have long trunks and large ears.

ostrich

I can see lots of different wild animals through my binoculars.

Make a line of lizards.

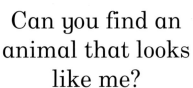

Can you find an animal that looks like me?

ROAR!

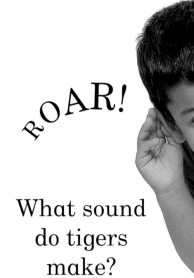

What sound do tigers make?

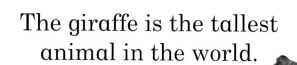
The giraffe is the tallest animal in the world.

Sea eagles swoop down and pluck fish from the water. Can you find any fish?

I'm hiding up a tree so that scary spider can't see me. But can you find scary spider?

All these mice are for my dinner.

My interesting face helps me to find a mate.

Find another mouse for the snake's dinner.

On the beach

Do you like to play in the sand and paddle in the sea?

The seagull is soaring in the wind.

Seals use their strong flippers to swim.

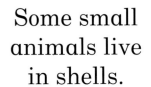

Some small animals live in shells.

Find a shell and a pebble to put on the sand.

Dolphins have fins as well as flippers.

A group of fish is called a school. Can you find some more fish?

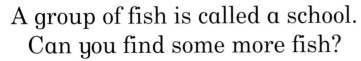

Starfish have five arms.

Nature's children

All these animals are young like me.

Where has mother duck gone?

Kittens grow very quickly.

I'm the younger kitten.

I'm the elder kitten.

A baby cow is called a calf.

Dogs grow quickly, too.

I'm the youngest puppy.

A baby rabbit is called a kitten.

Can you find a puppy who is older than me?

piglets suckling milk

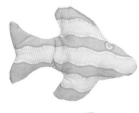

First published by Hermes House in 2002

© Anness Publishing Limited 2003

Hermes House is an imprint of
Anness Publishing Limited
Hermes House
88–89 Blackfriars Road
London SE1 8HA

A CIP catalogue for this book is available from the
British Library.

Publisher: Joanna Lorenz
Managing Editor, Children's Books: Gilly Cameron Cooper
Editors: Rebecca Clunes, Jennifer Davidson, Rasha Elsaeed,
Leon Gray, Jenni Rainford, Sarah Uttridge
Editorial Reader: Joy Wotton
Design: Mike Leaman, Sarah Melrose, Ann Samuel,
Simon Wilder, Roger McWilliam, Alix Wood
Jacket Design: Alix Wood of Applecart

Previously published in eight separate volumes
in the *Sticker Fun* series:
*Animal Friends, Babies and Toddlers, Clothes,
Food and Drink, My Day, My Home, Nature, Party*

The publishers would like to thank all the children
who appear in this book.

1 3 5 7 9 10 8 6 4 2

Stickers

page 6

page 7

page 8

page 9

page 10

page 11

page 12

page 13

page 14

page 15

page 16

page 17

page 18

page 19

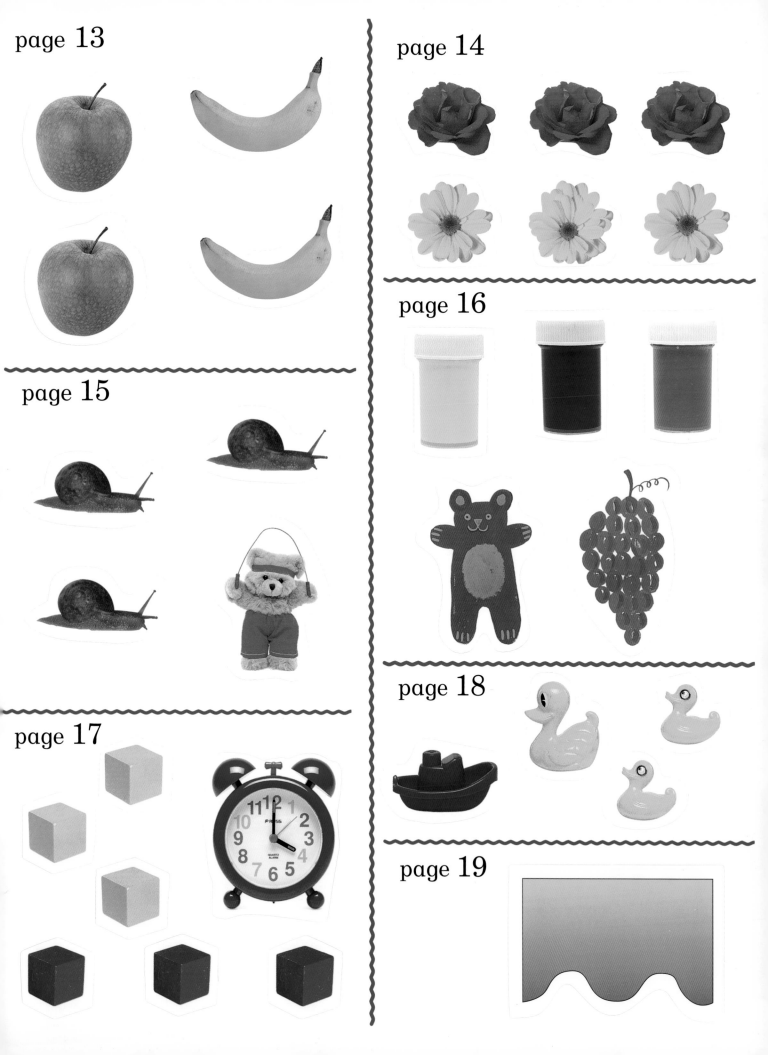

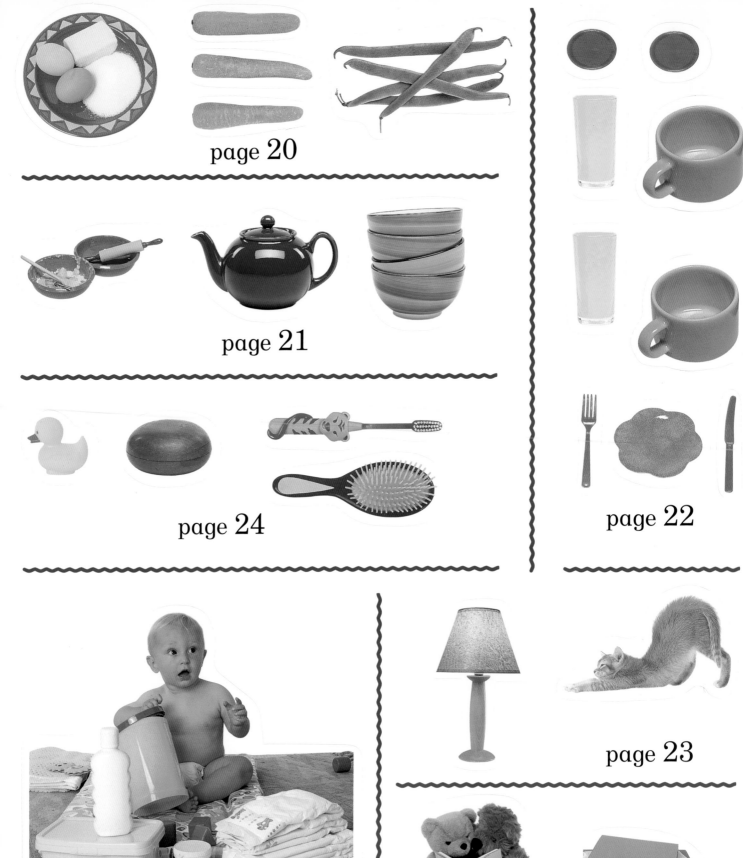

page 20

page 21

page 24

page 22

page 23

page 25

page 26

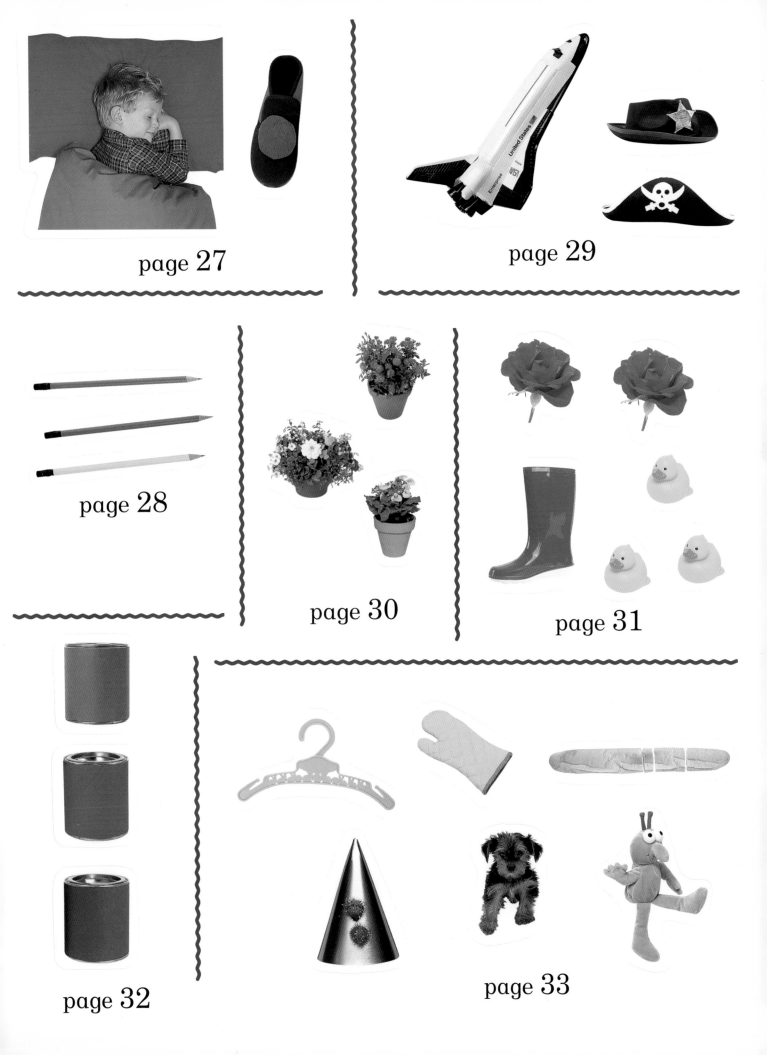

page 27

page 29

page 28

page 30

page 31

page 32

page 33

page 36

page 37

page 38

page 39

page 40

page 41

page 42

page 43

page 44

page 49

page 45

page 46

page 47

page 48

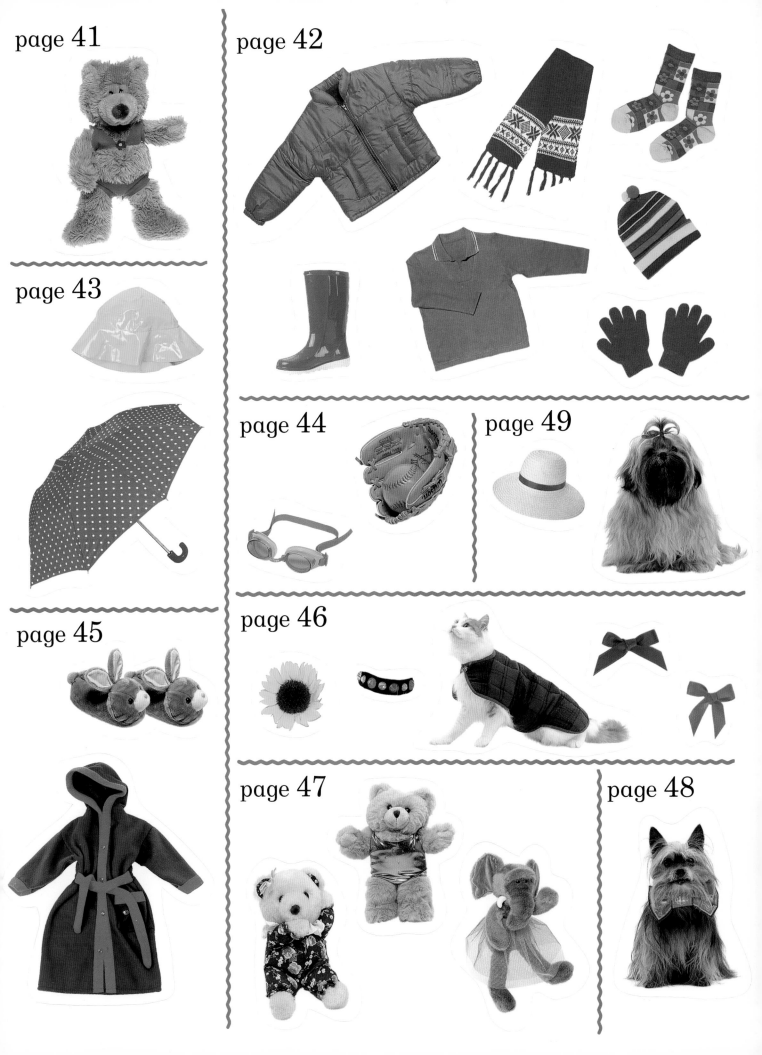

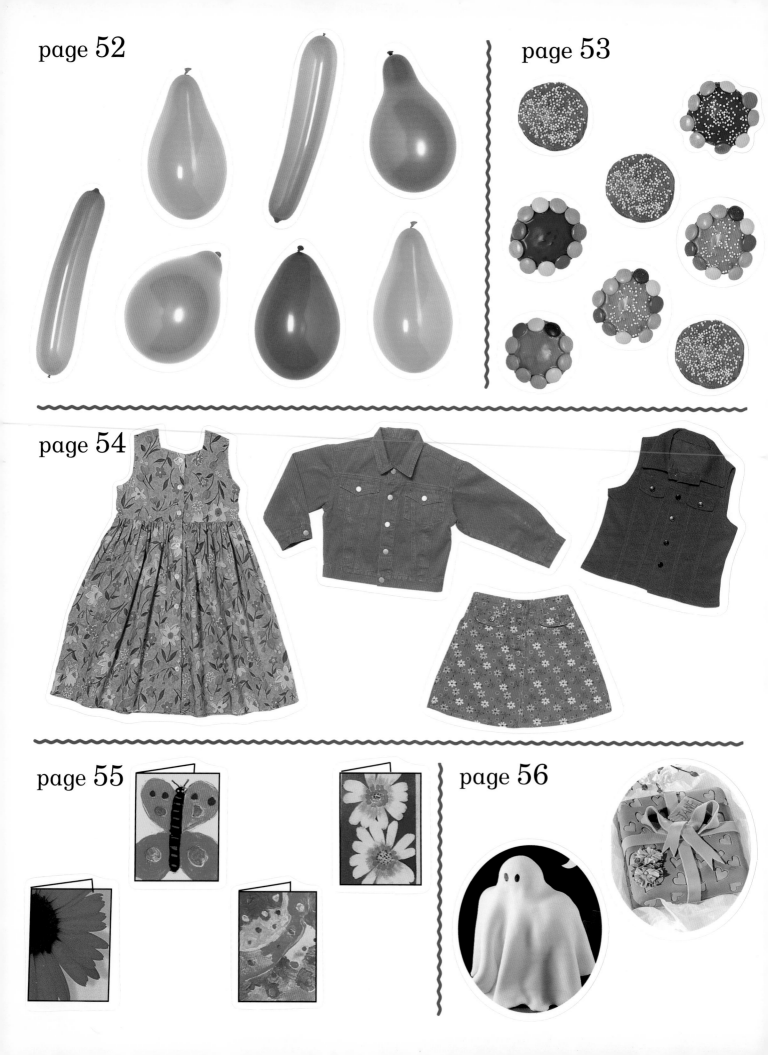

page 52

page 53

page 54

page 55

page 56

page 57

page 58

page 59

pages 60 and 61

pages 64 and 65

pages 62 and 63

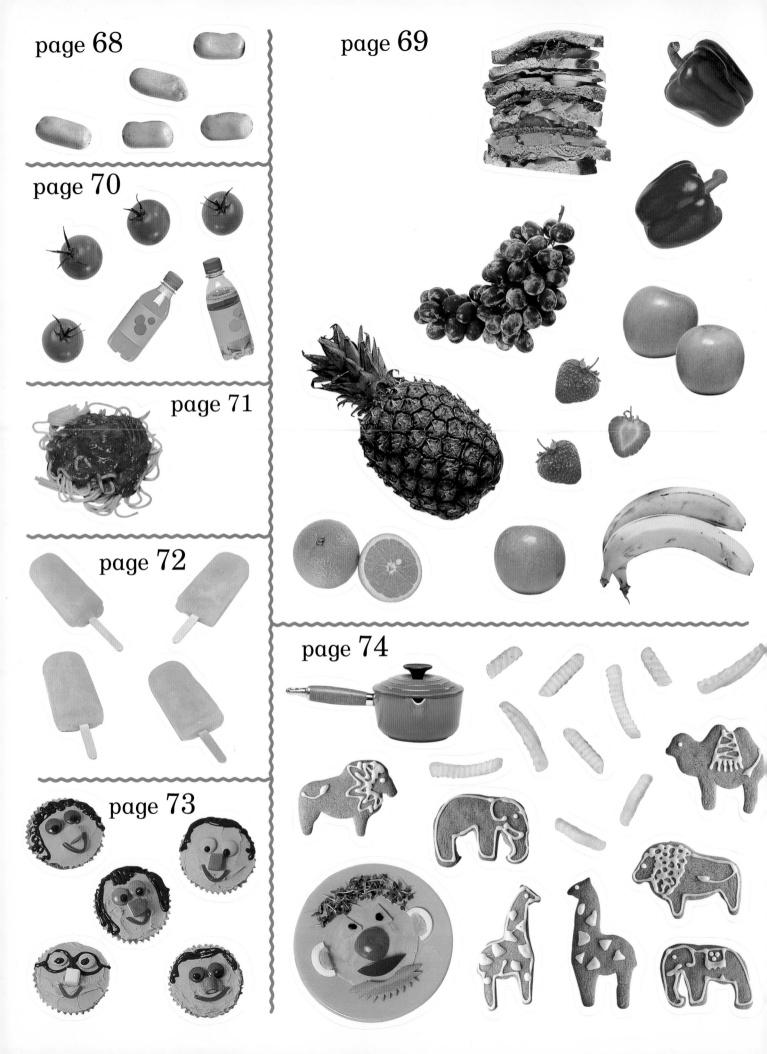

page 68

page 69

page 70

page 71

page 72

page 73

page 74

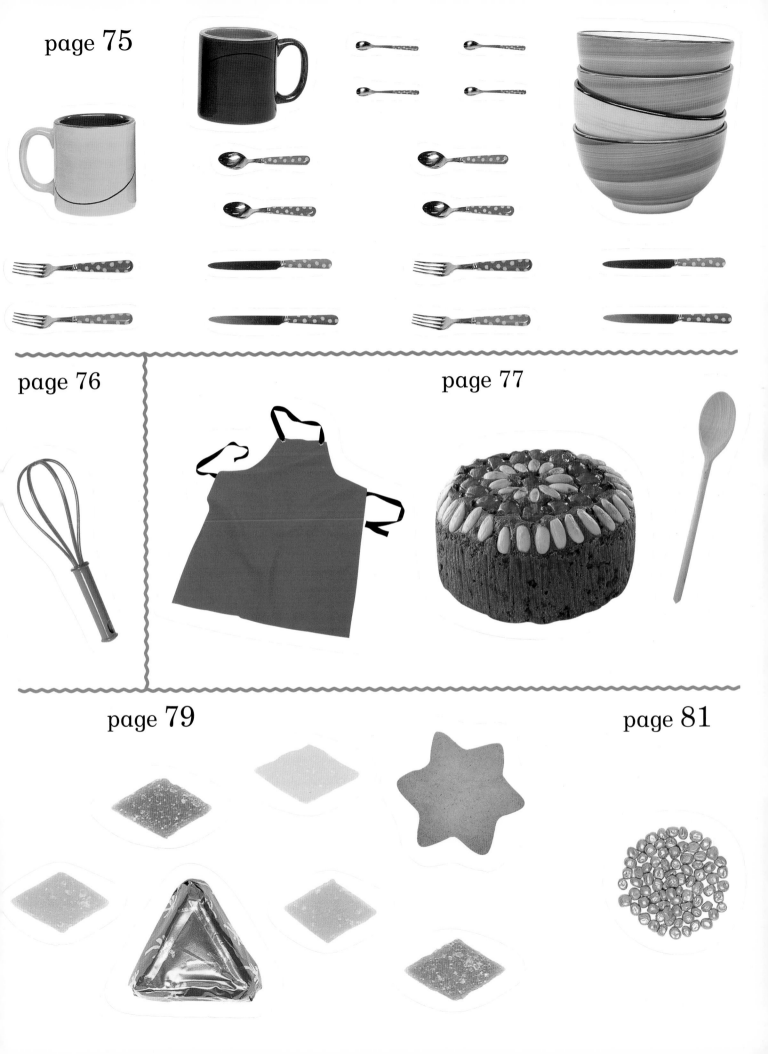

page 75

page 76

page 77

page 79

page 81

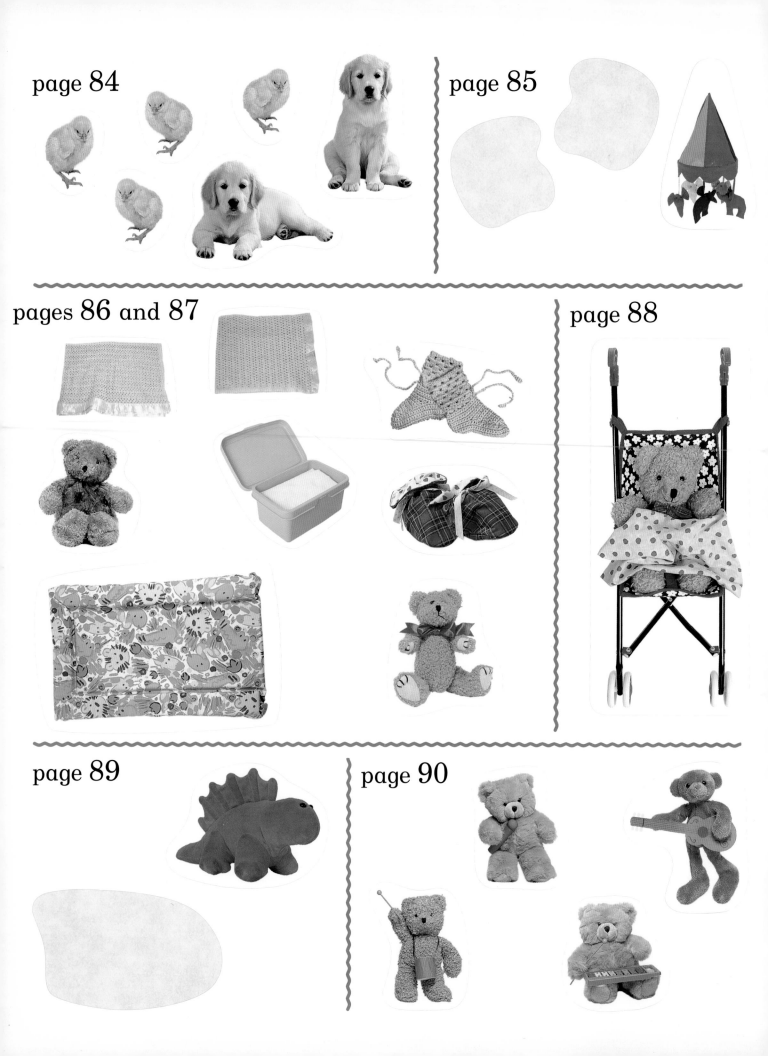

page 84

page 85

pages 86 and 87

page 88

page 89

page 90

page 91

page 92

page 93

page 94

page 95

page 96

page 97

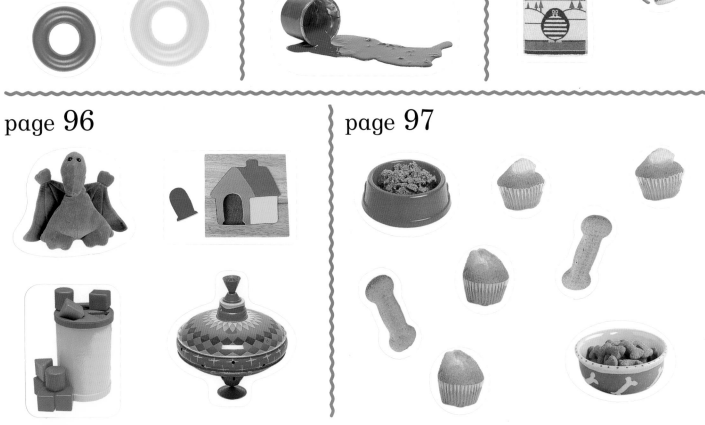

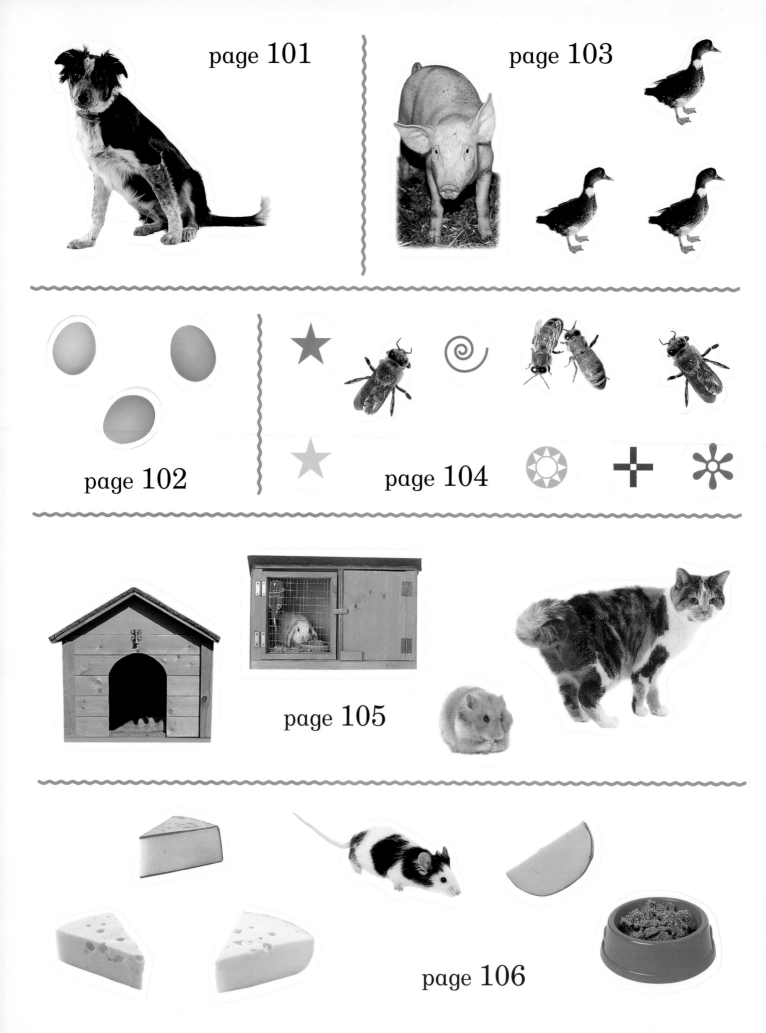

page 101

page 103

page 102

page 104

page 105

page 106

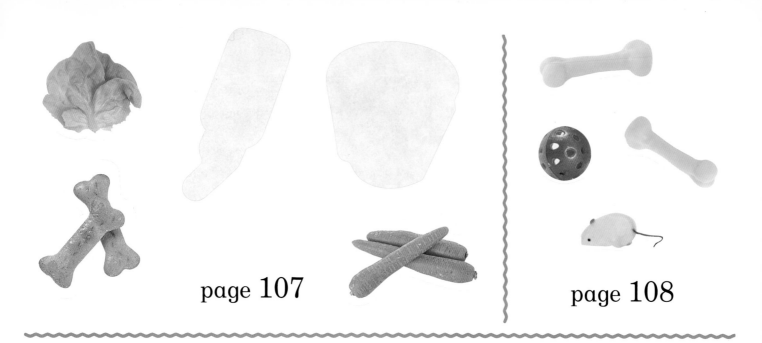

page 107

page 108

page 109

page 111

pages 112 and 113

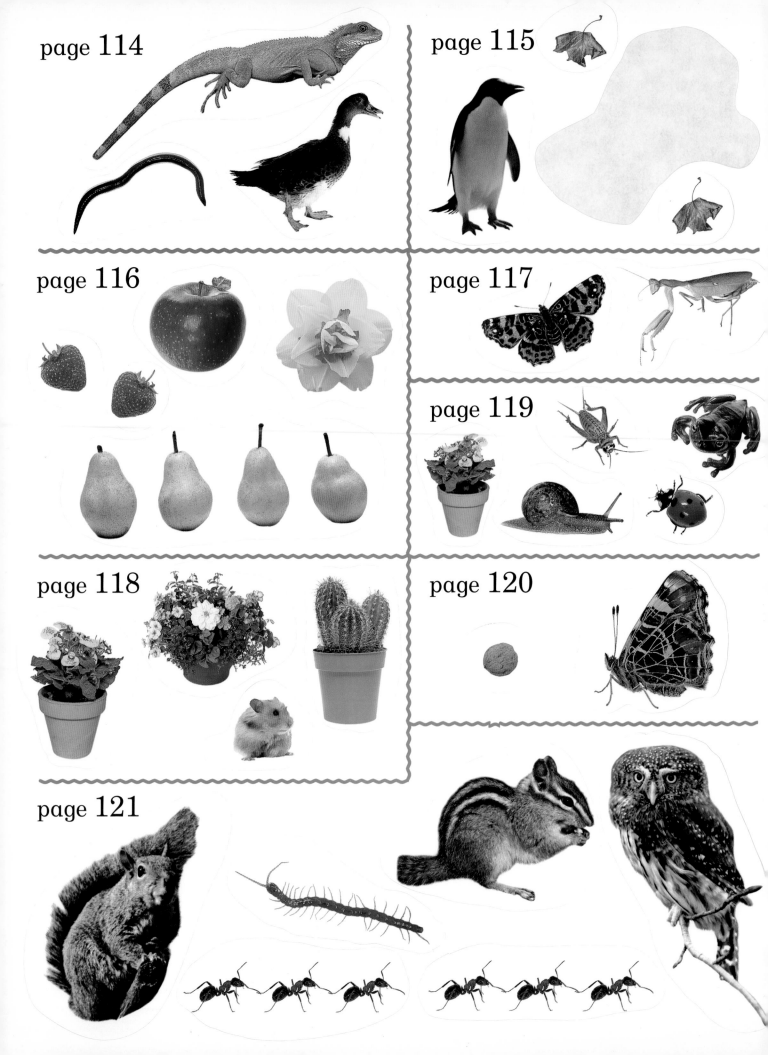

page 114

page 115

page 116

page 117

page 119

page 118

page 120

page 121

page 122

page 124

page 123

page 125

page 126

page 127